CW00471126

Polonius

1946-1958

Memories of a singular horse

Tim Hailstone

To Chris.

I hope you enjoy this slice of prehistoric rural life. At least, it won't take long to read!

As ever

[signature] February 2024

Polonius
1946-1958

Memories of a singular horse

©Tim Hailstone

First Edition 2020
Printed by Blissetts of London

ISBN 978-1-905912-71-1

A catalogue record of this book is
available from the British Library.

Introduction

Whether my friends will welcome this slim volume is open to question. They may feel that, over the years, they have heard quite enough from me about Polonius. However, two of them have long encouraged me to commit my memories of him to paper, so it is they who must take most of the blame.

Tim Cox possesses a huge knowledge about racing and equine matters generally and has assembled what must be the largest library of publications on those subjects. He is a veritable mine of information and has supplied me with indispensable source material and has confirmed or corrected many matters of historical fact. He even offered scholarly support for my preference for 'chesnut' over 'chestnut'.

Brough Scott is many things but, most of all, he is an enthusiast. Without his pep talks, conducted via Zoom in our respective gardens, I may never have put my shoulder to this wheel, even when confined to boring, racing-free barracks by the Coronavirus epidemic.

The first draft of this memoir was very much about Polonius and, of course, he remains at its heart. Since that first attempt, however, I have introduced much about the life of our family in south Leicestershire in the 1950s and the people who were in our lives. Tim and Brough both encouraged this development. I hope it makes the story a fuller and more interesting one.

Other friends who have helped me with their suggestions and corrections are David Ashforth, Farhad Dalal, Sean Magee, Chris Pitt, Graham Sharpe and Sandra Wake, but it goes without saying that the errors to be found within these pages are all my own work.

In the course of my publishing career, I observed that for an author to fail, extravagantly to thank his wife, is a social crime on a par with a politician failing to sport a poppy on Armistice Day, and I have often felt that such acknowledgements were perfunctory.

However, as an author for the first time, my expression of gratitude to Jenny comes from deep in my heart. There is no more precious quality than kindness, and she is, quite simply, the kindest person I have ever known. She had no interest in horses when we met but, in our dozen or so years together, has attended many race meetings and put up with much racing talk, largely without complaint.

The empty bridle

I was eleven and it was a bitterly cold day just before Christmas. I rode the chesnut gelding with the broad white blaze up the hill from the yard to the big flat field above the village. My father was on his hunter and when we reached the top we swapped mounts and I watched as he cantered and then galloped round the long skinny expanse of grass. Suddenly, on the second circuit, at the far end, they were on the ground. I kicked my horse hard all the way but by the time I got there, my father had the bridle in his hands and Polonius was breathing his last. There is nothing in my memories of early childhood that stands out like that scene. The horse dying before our eyes, my father, bereft, with tears on his cheeks, and the sad walk home with the empty bridle to break the dreadful news.

Belcher's Lodge

Our story with Polonius began five years earlier in 1953 in south Leicestershire.

Before the war my father had worked as agent for George Brudenell of Deene Park, Northamptonshire. He was very grand, being descended from the Lord Cardigan who led the Charge of the Light Brigade. The remains of Ronald, his charger, are buried under an oak tree in Deene Park. The Brudenells have lived at Deene Park without interruption for five hundred years. I encountered Mr Brudenell from time to time through my childhood and my teenage years. To a small boy, he was a little scary, a deeply eccentric Victorian squire, festooned with whiskers, clad in fairly archaic clothing and paranoid about germs. He would never handle cash and always had a glove in his right pocket, so as to avoid his skin coming into contact with door knobs and the like. By the time I was in my mid-teens, in the Sixties, he cut a very odd figure indeed.

Dad in the RAF in South Africa

Early in the war Dad went to London to try to get into the cavalry, but was turned down for the bizarre reason that he had flat feet. A little later, sometime in 1940, he joined the RAF at Lord's Cricket Ground and spent the rest of the war flying in bombers, first as a bomb aimer and later as pilot. Against the odds he survived and when he came home, with a Distinguished Flying Cross, Mr Brudenell, who was always fond of Dad, granted him the tenancy of one of his Leicestershire farms, Belcher's Lodge, near Horninghold, between Market Harborough and Uppingham.

Belcher's Lodge was by no means an easy billet. It was a rather drab and draughty house on a little used lane at the top of a steep hill and was a couple of miles from the nearest habitation. It was without electricity in our early years there, so my mother had to cook on an old black range and do her ironing using flat irons heated on it. After dark, we were lit by glass chimney oil lamps. Dad acquired a generator at the closing down sale of a US Army base but it was only used for milking. Electrical power to the house had to wait a few more years until the mains supply arrived.

Belcher's Lodge, where my family lived from 1946 to 1957, looking much more user friendly now than it was 65 years ago. The farm buildings have all been converted to dwellings.

Life at Belcher's Lodge was bucolic although, perhaps, not as perfectly pleasant as that description implies, but there was much fun for we children. My mother had no driving licence so local trips were taken by courtesy of a shaggy old mare named Kitty, in her trap. Butter was made every week in an old coopered churn with a winding handle and a little glass window for checking that it had set. We collected eggs from all over the farm, knowing each hen's favourite laying place. In the spring, in the kitchen and scullery, we raised cade lambs (as

The author's Coronation portrait 1953

orphan sheep are known in the East Midlands.) The day when Louise, my favourite, was taken to market was a tearful one and remains a sharp memory to this day.

We had a nice flock of Border Leicester ewes and, to keep them in order, a lovely Rough Collie bitch named, with no great originality, Lassie. My sister and I would stand either side of the bow top iron railings that stood between the house and the lane and call Lassie back and forth. She loved leaping over the railings. On one heart stopping occasion, she jumped a shade too low and got one of her front legs jammed through the bow. We ran to the fence, took her weight and yelled for my parents. Fortunately, Lassie emerged from this episode with a leg that was very sore but not broken.

Lassie was not allowed in the house. The only dog with that privilege was Gem, a Smooth Fox Terrier bitch. She was not an ideal pet for a family with young children. She liked playing but, if not in the mood, could be very irritable and even snappy. Until she died, my sister bore a scar on her temple where Gem had bitten her when she was very small. There was lots of blood. Nowadays the dog would probably have been put down. Gem was a great ratter and very proud of the results of her efforts. On many a morning outside the back door of the house there was a neat line of rat corpses. I often got the job of burying them at the far end of the orchard. Further evidence of Gem's rather uncompromising temperament is provided by her behaviour as a mother. On at least two occasions she found herself in the family way. When her time came she would disappear. A few days later, her puppies would be found dead on the cold ground. I suppose she couldn't be bothered with them.

My father and his brothers had all ridden and hunted from early childhood, although the Woodland Pytchley country where their father farmed in north-east Northamptonshire wasn't quite of the quality of neighbouring hunts such as the Cottesmore, Quorn and the Pytchley proper. At Belcher's Lodge we were in the middle of the Fernie, the kennels of which are at Great Bowden, just outside Market Harborough. Originally, the Fernie was a breakaway from the Quorn and its country had been much disputed but, by the Fifties, it was well established. The Fernie is the only hunt whose country is entirely within Leicestershire, the greatest hunting county. Colonels Derrick Hignett and Pen Lloyd were excellent Joint Masters in the post-war period and the rather volatile Yorkshireman, Walter Gupwell, was a vigorous and charismatic huntsman. We were enthusiastic members of the hunt and, as farmers in the country, we didn't have to pay a subscription. My father hunted a great deal, often in the company of Sidney Gent, one of our farmer neighbours. Mr Gent, who was in his late seventies, smoked a pipe that slipped from between his teeth several times most days. Dad's report on the day's sport, when he returned from hunting always included the number of times he had to dismount to recover Sidney's pipe. Mr Gent rarely got much further than the meet and when I started hunting (aged seven, I think), my father required me to be the picker up of the pipe and I was not allowed to continue my day's hunting until Sidney had retired from the fray. I, and later my sister, Vicky, too, were keen members of the Fernie Pony Club and we walked a pair of foxhound puppies every year. My favourite was Watchman and, when I was hunting, I could always pick him out of the pack.

Vicky and I astride Kitty with my older half-brother Simon at her head and Mum holding Watchman

My mother and grandmother with cade lambs, about 1926

Mum and Dad had courted, before the war, but my somewhat narrow-minded maternal grandmother, a former school mistress, disapproved of the Hailstone family. My paternal grandfather had had 'difficulties' with the Inland Revenue and my father and his brothers did quite a bit of drinking, crashing cars and getting into minor scrapes with the constabulary. Perhaps, not unreasonably, my grandmother was not keen for her daughter to marry into such a family. However, she was very impressed by a young Scots GP who had just moved to Corby, near where my mother's family lived. So, to my grandmother's satisfaction, her daughter became a doctor's wife.

Mum as a wartime nurse in VAD uniform

It was said locally that the young doctor was greatly loved by his patients, but he was a heavy drinker who became rather unpleasant when drunk. At the end of the war my mother who had been nursing as a member of the Voluntary Aid Detachment at the vast military hospital at Netley near Southampton, decided not to return to her husband and went to live with Dad at Belcher's Lodge. My mother's divorce, on grounds of her adultery, was granted in 1947. She and my father married immediately, but I have never established whether the ceremony took place before or after I arrived. I suppose it always felt like a rather indelicate question to ask. I don't think I particularly wish to know now.

Mum survived Dad (who died at 59) by more than a third of a century, so she had plenty of time to reminisce about him. She often recalled those early years of their marriage in Leicestershire. She felt that, although my father disliked the discipline and the many pointless rules and regulations to which he was subject in the RAF and, although he was keen to get out of uniform at the end of the war, he found farming rather dull and humdrum, after being aircrew for four years. She believed that was the main reason he took to riding in point-to-points with such enthusiasm. He had a fair bit of success, riding winners at Garthorpe, Guilsborough and Dingley. On one occasion he went as far as Yorkshire to win an important open race with Sergeant Pilot, a bay gelding, who was the best pointer we had. The pointers my father rode must have carried a fair bit of lead, because he was slim and wiry man who could do ten and a half stone and even a few pounds less, with a few days wasting.

Haymaking at Belcher's Lodge with my sister, mother, grandmother and dogs, including the eccentric Gem

People

When my father took the tenancy on Belcher's Lodge, my mother was still extricating herself from her first marriage, so he was living there alone at first. In the nearby village of Horninghold there was a Post Office that also sold newspapers and tobacco. It was kept by a Glaswegian woman, Agnes Inchley. She had been in service at Horninghold Hall and had married a local man, Ben Inchley. He was quite young when he died, and she became Horninghold's post mistress, which position provided her with a living and a home for her and her young son, Archie. The house was not built to be a shop and Mrs Inchley conducted business in what would otherwise have been the sitting room of her cottage.

The 'garden village' of Horninghold

Dad used to go down to Mrs Inchley's most days for his Player's and the Daily Express, the paper of choice in our house largely because of the presence of Peter O'Sullevan and Clive Graham in its pages. Mrs Inchley always had a pot of usually rather stewed tea on the go and, one day, over a cup of it, she told my father that her son, Archie, was about to leave hospital and that she had to arrange a taxi to bring him home. Archie had been a stoker on Ark Royal where he developed TB. He had been cured at Yardley Green Sanatorium in east Birmingham and was ready to return to civilian life.

Of course, Dad immediately offered to fetch Archie from Birmingham. A few days later, they met for the first time outside the hospital and became lifelong friends.

Archie was a gregarious character of an entrepreneurial bent. He expanded Mrs Inchley's business by delivering newspapers to half a dozen local villages and also distributed medicines for Dr Pickering, the GP in nearby Hallaton. For years he did this all on a big Norton motor bike until he acquired a van in the late Fifties. As quite a small boy, going on Archie's rounds with him was hugely exciting. I don't think he ever possessed a crash helmet and I certainly never wore one.

Archie never sat astride a horse but he was a keen racegoer and he soon introduced my parents to the local 'horsey' pub, the Royal Oak, which was in Hallaton, a village of about five hundred souls a mile or so beyond Horninghold. Hallaton had three pubs, the Fox, the Bewicke Arms, which are still open, and the Oak, which closed its doors some time ago.

The Old Royal Oak in Hallaton

The Royal Oak hardly conformed to the modern idea of a country inn. It was not at all picturesque and had a generally quite shabby air. The brick façade was on Hallaton's High Street. Those driving for a drink turned right into Hog Lane and from there into the pub's yard, which held pigs and horses, as well as customers' cars.

The landlord was a rather bad-tempered widower from Yorkshire named Bob Noble. He ran the pub with his two daughters, Joyce and Glenna. They also raised weaners and dealt in horses and ponies. The girls were both good riders and did a lot of show jumping and point-to-pointing, which they used as a showcase for their current stock. Glenna's fiancé, Jack Mason, another local farmer, was a very good and active point-to-point rider. I think Dad's first point-to-point rides may have been on Noble horses and Vicky and I often rode their ponies at gymkhanas.

Bob Noble used to go up north buying horses and ponies, often at horse fairs. Sometimes Dad would go with him and they would buy stock together. The results of such purchases were often stabled at Belcher's Lodge. They usually arrived by train at Hallaton station which was outside the village, on the road to Horninghold, a bit less than two miles from Belcher's Lodge. Hallaton was on both the Market Harborough to Nottingham and the Leicester to Peterborough lines.

The station had stabling for two horses. From about the age of seven I often went down to the station on my bike to bring these purchases home. If they weren't rideable, I would lead them through Horninghold and up Belcher's Hill. Dad would pick my bike up on his way home from the Oak.

The station staff were always kind and helpful. Sid Reade was the porter cum signalman. He would help me tack up. The stationmaster was Mr Gittins, a somewhat forbidding figure but with a motherly wife who used to give me pop and cakes. Sid worked at the station before the war and often spoke of Reynoldstown boarding the train at Hallaton en route to Aintree for his National wins in 1935 and 1936. His owner, Major Noel Furlong, trained him under a permit at Skeffington Hall only seven miles from Hallaton.

Like Polonius, Reynoldstown was also flat bred. His sire, My Prince was moderately successful at middle distances on the flat and then became a champion National Hunt sire, his progeny winning the Grand National four times in nine years with Gregalach (1929) Reynoldstown (1935/36), and Royal Mail(1937). Also, like Polonius, Reynoldstown suffered serious leg problems following his first National. Major Furlong's recipe was not cold water but 'time, tar and tarmac' – coating his legs with tar plus lots of road work.

Joyce Noble, Bob's elder daughter, became a close friend of my mother, and even taught her to ride a bit. Joyce was a very pretty, amusing and affectionate woman, who, although outwardly cheerful, harboured a deep sadness that she could not have the man she desired. Why she wanted him was a mystery. Tom Johnson, another farmer, was a grossly fat and quite boorish individual, who was said to be one of the least popular members of the Royal Oak crowd. Joyce's regular consort at social events was different altogether. Geoff Allingham, a feed salesman, was extremely funny and charming, and greatly loved by we children, because he made time for us and played pranks. I think that one would have applied to him that euphemism of the time, 'a confirmed bachelor'.

Mum and Dad with Joyce Noble and her regular dance partner, Geoff Allingham

The only celebrity who regularly visited the Royal Oak was Jack Gardner. Gardner, yet another local farmer, was a flashily handsome man, with a touch of Errol Flynn about him, who had become Army and

Imperial Services heavyweight champion boxer and gone on to claim the ABA title while doing his National Service in the Grenadier Guards shortly after the War. In 1950, he took the British and Empire crown from Bruce Woodcock at Earl's Court and became European champion the year after. In 1950s rural Leicestershire that made him a big star and the pub was always buzzing when Jack was there. We used to listen to his fights on the wireless. When asked by Eamonn Andrews or W Barrington Dalby if he would like to send a message to those at

Jack Gardner, champion heavyweight boxer

home, he would always say 'Love to Grace and Jim and all at Market Harborough' in a broad East Midlands accent.

Dad greatly enjoyed being in licensed premises and another favourite of his was the Vaults in Uppingham in the county of Rutland, less than five miles from Belcher's Lodge. One could ride to Uppingham avoiding the public highway almost entirely, so he often went there on horseback. Stockeston Hill, about half way, was very steep and the road formed a large zigzag. One lunchtime in the Vaults my father and another customer got into an argument about who could get down Stockeston Hill quicker, Dad on his horse or the other chap in his van. A wager was struck (and probably side bets too) and the company decamped to the top of the hill, about a mile and a half away, where the race was to start. The finishing line was to be the bridge over the Eye Brook in the valley below. My father jumped his horse from the road into a field. At the bottom he jumped back onto the road, then into the next field and won comfortably.

A raucous crowd returned to Belcher's Lodge to celebrate this great victory. Among them was a man wearing a dinner jacket. His name was Bert Wilson and he was the owner of the Rutland Cinema in

Uppingham. Those managing cinemas routinely wore dinner jackets - up until the Sixties, I think. There is an incident featuring Bert Wilson, the memory of which I treasure. Dad was not a film fan but every year went to see the Pathé News film of the Grand National. On one such occasion, with me in tow, my father had got the time of the showing of the National wrong and we arrived to the bad news that the race had already been shown. Reluctant to disappoint us, after a moment of thought, Bert Wilson said 'There are not many in there Colin. Go on in and I'll run it again.'

Another of those celebrating Dad's triumph on Stockeston Hill was George Burnham.

George Burnham

His land ran next to ours but, whereas we were on the hill above the village, he was in Horninghold where Mrs Inchley had her Post Office. It was an unusual and rather odd village. At the beginning of the 20th century, a man named Hardcastle had purchased the entire Horninghold estate and turned it into a 'garden village'. He built ironstone, brick and half-timbered houses in a neat and symmetrical pattern and surrounded them with ornamental shrubs and a variety of trees. More of the houses in Horninghold were grand that were humble. Some were what would now be called second homes. They had stabling and were used by their owners from Leicester, Birmingham or even London, as bases from which to hunt with the fashionable shire packs.

George Burnham lived in Orchard House, a red brick house with a Queen Anne façade, a fairly grand stable yard with a fountain and about 200 acres. Although from a respectable East Midlands farming family, Burnham did not look or act much like a farmer. He sported a handlebar, Jimmy Edwards style moustache and tended to wear rather loud tweeds. His manner was that of the better class of salesman

Orchard House, Horninghold, home of George Burnham

and, indeed, he ended his working life as the owner of a garage (to which he seemed much more suited than farming). In short, George Burnham was something of a caricature.

Those who might form the impression that Burnham had seen active service were not discouraged from that assumption but he had been in a non-combat role in the RAF and possessed little courage. Only the most placid of horses failed to intimidate him and he generally gave them a wide berth. On one occasion he and Dad took a couple of horses to south Devon in August. There was a couple of days to kill between Buckfastleigh and Newton Abbot meetings and they decided to pay Torquay a visit. They got on a double decker bus and Dad headed for the front seats on the upper deck. Courteously, he offered George the seat next to the window, so that he could enjoy the view. At one point on their journey the ground fell away sharply at the side of the road. Burnham turned white as a sheet and insisted on returning to the lower deck.

My father thought Burnham a rather preposterous character but he also found him entertaining and was, perhaps, attracted to him in that way that rather shy men are sometimes drawn to more voluble ones. They did quite a lot of drinking together, went to the fights at Leicester's De Montfort Hall and also went racing at Leicester, Huntingdon and Towcester, and sometimes further afield to Cheltenham and Sandown.

It was George Burnham who did us the great service of bringing Polonius into our lives.

Antecedents and Newmarket origins

While this is primarily intended as a personal memoir of those years in which Polonius was a member of our family, it would not be complete without a brief account of his earlier history. Researching those years has introduced me to some important and interesting horses and men of the turf.

Polonius was bred, probably in Newmarket, by Alexander R Cox. A R Cox inherited his thoroughbred interests from his older brother Alfred W Cox who died in 1919. They were the sons of a Liverpool jute merchant. After Malvern, Alfie's family wanted him to go into the army. When he disappointed them by failing to be accepted by the Royal Military Academy at Woolwich, they gave him £100 and dispatched him to Australia. On the voyage there, playing cards, he won a share in a run-down sheep station. There turned out to be a huge amount of silver beneath the grazing sheep. The site became the famous Broken Hill silver mine and made Alfie Cox extremely wealthy.

It is said that when he returned to London he devoted the remaining thirty years of his life to Havana cigars, old brandy and blood-stock. For some reason, never divulged, he adopted the *nom de course* of Mr Fairie. One feels that it would hardly be the nickname of choice for a racing man, nowadays. He is said to have been a brusque, strong willed and uncompromising individual who despised the social graces and didn't care much that he wasn't very popular.

Mr Fairie's interest in breeding and racing was very fruitful indeed. He sent his well-bred mare Isoletta to Galopin, the 1895 Derby winner and sire of St Simon. The result was Galicia. She won

A. W. Cox 'Mr Fairie'

as a two-year-old but broke down the following season and was retired for breeding, at which she was a huge success. She produced four winners of 42 races including Bayardo and Lemberg, two of the best-known racehorses of the early twentieth century, and who gave Alfie Cox victories in the Derby, the St Leger, two Eclipses and three Champion Stakes. At stud, Bayardo sired Gay Crusader, who won a wartime Triple Crown in 1917 (when all three races took place at Newmarket.) When he died and passed on his financial and equine fortune to his brother, A W Cox had won all five Classics, including the Derby and the St Leger twice.

Little is known of Alexander Cox, other than his continuation of his brother's bloodstock activities, but the impression is of a quieter, less flamboyant man. He took over his brother's colours and his position as principal patron of the Manton stables of the younger Alec Taylor. Although he operated on a somewhat more modest scale than his brother, he still bred horses that won him 77 races before he died in 1950.

One of those horses was Polonius.

Alexander Cox bred Polonius's dam, Charmian, from Ciceronetta, a mare that he had inherited from his brother. Like her son, Charmian was a chesnut. He and Alec Taylor must have thought she had some potential, because at two, she ran in the Richmond Stakes at Goodwood and in Kempton's International Plate, but she was unplaced in all of her four races that season. She continued racing over sprint trips at three and won a maiden plate at Salisbury in May 1935, her only racing victory. Upped in trip, she was ridden by Steve Donoghue in the Britannia Stakes at Royal Ascot. but was unplaced. Donoghue finished second on her in the Girton Handicap over 7 furlongs on the July Course at Newmarket and she was also runner up in the Leicestershire Oaks over 10 furlongs. She signed off her racing career in November, finishing second in a handicap over the Ditch Mile at Newmarket.

Charmian's sire, Pommern, was bred by Solly Joel whose nephew, Jim Joel, was to become one of only four owners to have won the Derby (with Royal Palace) and the Grand National (with Maori Venture) - and whose memorial trophy my racing partner and I won at Newbury with Filbert a few years ago. Pommern was very high class, winning a wartime Triple Crown in 1915.

Charmian did not have a happy time at stud. She was barren to a number of her suitors, slipped one foal and another was born dead close to term. She only produced two named offspring, Squadron Leader by Wychwood Abbot in 1939 and Polonius in 1946. In 1948, at the age 16, she was killed by lightning.

Polonius owed the first syllable of his name to Charmian's grandsire, Polymelus, who was a very influential stallion, siring the winners of seven Classics. Charmian herself probably also contributed to his name. Shakespeare's Charmian is a servant cum adviser to Cleopatra in the way that Polonius is to Claudius, Hamlet's antagonist.

Polonius's sire, Epigram, was by Son-in-Law, an outstanding performer over cup distances, winning the Goodwood Cup, the Jockey Club Cup (twice) and the Cesarewitch. He would very probably have won the Ascot Gold Cup but it was not run in WWI, when he was competing. He proved to be even more important when he went to stud, siring the winners of four Ascot Gold Cups. When he published his *Peerage of Racehorses* in 1994, Richard Ulbrich described him as 'one of the principal influences for stamina in the modern thoroughbred'.

Epigram was bought for 4,500 guineas, as a yearling, by James Voase Rank. He was the brother who stayed with the family's milling business, while the younger J Arthur Rank went off, made movies and became the man behind, if not actually banging, the gong. (I don't suppose that J Arthur would be very thrilled to know that he has passed into the language as a particularly vulgar example of Cockney rhyming slang.)

J V Rank was a very successful businessman. He transformed his father's flour mill in Hull into a company that dominated its industry (and eventually became Rank Hovis McDougall.) Indeed, in World War II Rank was the man who was principally responsible for the nation's daily bread. As well as racing, under both codes, he was very interested in and knowledgeable about breeding Great Danes and Irish Wolfhounds and also beef cattle. He was on the Waterloo Committee of the National Coursing Club and in 1941 co-founded the Racehorse Owners Association. J V Rank was, most definitely, one of the great and the good. It is a little surprising that he was not elected to the Jockey Club until shortly before his death. Maybe having a fortune derived from trade still put them off at that time.

He won two Classics – the 1938 St Leger with Scottish Union and the 1943 Oaks with Why Hurry. He also had many National Hunt successes, including the Cheltenham Gold Cup in 1946 with the eleven-year-old Prince Regent, whom he had bought as a yearling. He never fulfilled his ambition to win a Grand National, although Cooleen was second and fourth, and Prince Regent was third and fourth.

Rank purchased the Druid's Lodge estate on Salisbury Plain the same year that he acquired the yearling Epigram, and sent him there to be handled by his private trainer, Noel Cannon. Epigram's career may perhaps be taken as sign that James Rank was a patient man. After a single race as a two-year-old and six more at three he had hardly earned a penny. However, he showed more promise when moved up to middle distances. In 1937, when he was four, he was stepped up again and, from July that year, ran all his races over at least 14 furlongs. He won eight of his fifteen races at three and four and ended his racing career winning the Queen Alexandra Stakes, the Goodwood Cup and the Doncaster Cup over a three-month period.

In his last five races, he was ridden by Bernard 'Brownie' Carslake who, after leaving his native Australia, had ridden in Austria-Hungary and Russia. He was champion jockey in Russia in 1916. The following year, when the 1917 Revolution kicked off, he fled to England, where he won seven Classics before he died in 1941.

Epigram was registered as brown and there is an oil painting of him entitled *Epigram, a brown racehorse with jockey up.* It is the work of Thomas Percy Earl. He was from a large family of sporting and animal painters and is recognised as one of the best horse painters of the period. He never exhibited his work, doing very well from commissions. It is reasonable to assume that this picture was commissioned by James V Rank in the wake of Epigram's successful five-year-old season. The rider, in Rank's silks, is probably Brownie Carslake.

Epigram and his son, Polonius, shared two striking attributes. Both performed best over staying trips and both took years to show their best ability. Epigram showed himself to be an outstanding stayer only when he was five. When Polonius won a chase over 25 furlongs at Newton Abbot in August 1955 he was nine, and his only previous victory was in a ten-furlong handicap on the flat at Nottingham, when he was three.

Epigram painted by Thomas Percy Earl. The rider is probably Brownie Carslake

Alexander Cox continued to be a major patron of the Manton stables after Alec Taylor Jr's retirement in 1927, when Joe Lawson, Taylor's assistant, took over. Joe Lawson was Manton's master for almost twenty years. Only about a year or so before he moved to Newmarket, he gave his first racing job to young Eugene Kelly, who, about ten years later, was to ride Polonius in the Grand National.

When Joe Lawson took up residence at the Carlburg Stables on Newmarket's Bury Road (now Roger Varian's base) one of the first horses he received, from Alexander Cox, was two-year-old Polonius.

It seems likely that, given Polonius's breeding, Cox and Lawson hardly expected him to win his two-year-old outings over sprint trips, a view supported by his odds of 33/1 in two big fields and 100/8 when there were eight runners. In one of these races he was ridden by Doug Smith's brother, Eph.

For his seasonal debut race at three years in 1949, a handicap over a mile and a quarter at Nottingham, Eph Smith was again his jockey. This was quite a valuable race, with a purse of £708 (about £25,000 in 2020) and Polonius was fancied this time. He opened as 2/1 favourite before drifting out to 3s, as money came for Ordnance, ridden by apprentice Carol Orton (not a lady rider!), who started at 11/4. Polonius was waited with, fifth of the eight runners, turning for home and, in the final furlong, overhauled Garter Knight to win by three quarters of a length. The runner-up was ridden by Bill Rickaby, Lester Piggott's cousin.

Sixteen days later, in another valuable handicap over a mile and a half on the Cesarewitch course at Newmarket, Polonius started clear favourite at 100/30 with Michael Beary, close to the end of his riding career, in the saddle. Held up again, he was ridden three furlongs out, finishing fourth, four and a half lengths behind the winner, giving between 10 and 16 pounds to the horses in front of him.

Polonius's final outing for A R Cox and Joe Lawson was in a marathon handicap over two miles and two furlongs on St Leger Day at Doncaster. He was easy to back at 100/7, finishing sixth, eleven lengths behind the winner. He was ridden by 20-year-old apprentice, Willie Snaith, who was to live a long life, only dying in June 2019 at the age of 91 .

Polonius embarks on a National Hunt career

According to George Burnham, Polonius was badly lame after the Doncaster race and proved to have sustained a fairly severe suspensory injury to his nearside front leg. He didn't see a racecourse again for eighteen months by which time he was owned by Burnham.

In 1951, Polonius was five and was to be found in the stables of Ralph Smalley Tebbutt, with Burnham as registered owner. I don't remember Tebbutt but I recall my father mentioning him without enthusiasm. I have the impression that he was rather in the Burnham mould but without the saloon bar charm.

Tebbutt's stables were at Foxton, on the Leicester side of Market Harborough, about ten miles from Belcher's Lodge. He held a licence for four seasons, during which time he was at three different yards, the last, in the 1954-55 season, being at Wiseton, near Doncaster. During those four years he never had more than ten horses in his care and had only one winner.

It is not clear exactly when Polonius left Ralph Tebbutt but, by the end of 1951, he was at Orchard House, Horninghold with George Burnham, who was granted a permit to train at some point that year. This was hardly an encouraging development, as Burnham had a poor understanding of horses and, indeed, gave the impression that they frightened him.

Tebbutt had not done very well with the horse but he kept him busy. During 1951 he ran in six flat races and ten over hurdles. In most of his flat races, mainly sellers (races in which the winner is auctioned immediately after the race) over long trips, he started at 20/1 or longer and was never very close to being in the money. He fared a little better in his hurdle races, managing two fourths and a third (at Doncaster), over two and a half miles or more. He never started at shorter than 10/1. The courses at which he competed included Lincoln, Birmingham and Manchester, at all of which, horse racing ended more than fifty years ago.

The rider who was on him in most of his National Hunt races in 1951 was Derek Leslie. He was 22 then, a local lad from Melton Mowbray. I remember seeing him ride often at Towcester, Huntingdon and Leicester in my adolescence. He rode 173 winners before he retired in the early Sixties. He was fifth on Sanperion in the 1954 Grand National, won by Royal Tan, the second of Vincent O'Brien's 1953-55 hat trick of National victories.

When Polonius was at Orchard House, only a couple of miles from Belcher's Lodge, my father started riding him out regularly. My mother recalled that he took a strong liking to Polonius from the first time he got on his back. Dad often accompanied him to the races, too. By 1952, Polonius was six and started chasing. He ran in seven races, but four were well short of three miles, which we later came to regard as his minimum trip. Derek Leslie rode him in most of his races and again a third and two fourths were his best results. In his last two races in 1952, in September and October, he was sent out to run on hard and firm ground, which seems to have been an odd decision for a horse with his medical history. After the second of these races, at Uttoxeter, he was very lame and it seems that his suspensory injury may have recurred.

The benefits of cold water

About ten years ago, not all that long before she died, I had a lengthy conversation with my mother about what happened next. Her recollection was that, after a lengthy period of box rest, followed by walking to hand and then being ridden at walking pace, as soon as Polonius was galloped, he went lame again.

My father often spoke about his grandfather's views on how to treat horses with fragile legs. I remember my great grandfather, Thomas, quite well. He lived until I was about five years old, well into his nineties. He had been a farmer all his life. I used to sit with him by the fire in the parlour at Carberry Farm, my grandfather's farm in Bulwick in east Northamptonshire. He used to spit into the fire quite often, which I found rather shocking and which disgusted my mother.

He talked about horses a lot, especially working horses. Much of his farming career had taken place before even steam traction engines were used on farms. He also spoke about racing. He told me that he had seen Fred Archer ride at Newmarket. At the time, I had no idea

My paternal great grandfather, Thomas Hailstone, showing off a parrot mouthed horse

who Fred Archer was but his name stuck in my memory and, years later, I realised that he and my great grandfather must have been born about the same time. In his earlier years, Thomas farmed just south of March, which is only about 25 miles from Newmarket, so he could easily have seen Fred ride there.

My great grandfather believed that the way to get a horse with swollen, inflamed cannon bones, fetlocks or pasterns, sound was to treat him with lots of very cold water and, if you valued the horse, to give him lots of time to recover before beginning to get him fit. On his farm there was a cold, fast running stream that was usually not too deep. He would put a stall in the stream and tether the affected horse there for a couple of hours or so every day, over many weeks.

Mum told me that Dad often said that he would love to see how Polonius would respond to this regime.

By the middle of 1953, it seems that George Burnham was getting very frustrated with Polonius's lack of progress.

£25 and a cartload of hay

My father always preferred driving but one afternoon in the autumn of 1953, he walked the two miles to Orchard House. A couple of hours or so later, he walked back up the hill leading a chesnut horse with a broad white blaze. He had bought Polonius for £25 and a cartload of hay.

Dad always gave the impression that he thought he had done a pretty keen deal but the record shows that at the October 1950 Tattersalls sale George Burnham paid £25 guineas, so in fact, he had made a profit of a load of hay less £1.25! £25 in 1953 would be worth £700 today, so Dad paid the equivalent of getting on for £1000 for this broken-down horse.

The yard in which we kept ponies and horses at Belcher's Lodge was definitely more farm than stable yard. It was shared with our milking herd of Friesians and, under foot, one usually felt mud rather than flag or cobblestones. At one end stood a double-decker bus. This had been converted into distinctly ramshackle living quarters for the various farm labourers that we employed from time to time. The first was a German prisoner of war named Horst. When I was older, I discovered that my parents often left Vicky and me in Horst's care when they went to the Oak. In later years I teased them about surrendering us to the enemy! When Polonius arrived, the bus was occupied by a very nice man, named Bill Ledbetter, who had a little experience with horses and got on well with Polonius.

Polonius's leg was hosed with very cold water twice a day for about an hour over many months, with 'blister' ointment applied under heavy bandages at night. I was often the one holding the hose. To do it, I used to sit on a milking stool. He was a generally well-mannered horse but he didn't greatly care for the sensation of the cold water running down his legs. I discovered that the best way to get him to stand still for the treatment was to start down at his fetlock and gradually to move the jet of water up his leg. Cold water running down an already cold leg seemed to irritate him less than when the leg was warm.

I cannot recall for how many months the cold water treatment continued. Each session seemed to me like an age to a small boy with a short attention span. Time is rather elastic when one is six. The day when my father cantered him was memorable. That would have been in the late spring of 1954, I think.

The first run under our ownership was in October of that year, almost exactly two years after his last race for George Burnham. It was a three-mile selling chase at Market Rasen. His rider was Tommy Shone, quite a successful journeyman jockey in the post-war period. A couple of weeks later, Derek Leslie rode him in a three mile handicap chase at Towcester.

Why my father didn't ride him in those first two come-back races, I

Vicky and I watching Mum hose Polonius's leg

Vicky and I with Polonius ready to take some exercise

don't know. Maybe he wasn't yet confident of his ability to compete against professionals or maybe it was the weights, at 10-4 and 10-5 (although he made 10-4 on a couple of subsequent occasions). He was pulled up on both of those outings and was then off for another six months. That may imply a setback with his leg or maybe Dad wanted to run him on better ground because those first two outings were on soft and heavy.

Vicky and I with Bill Ledbetter
watching our father on Polonius

1955 – rebirth of a racehorse

At all events, when he ran at Uttoxeter on 28th May 1955, with my father on him for the first time, he was nine years old and could hardly be said to have had a glittering career. He had competed in 14 flat and 20 National Hunt races and had recorded a single victory, six years previously.

What happened over the next seven months was scarcely short of miraculous. By the time Polonius turned ten, my father had ridden him in sixteen steeplechases, mainly over three miles, and he won five of them, was second four times and third three times.

At Newton Abbot, in August 1955, he was first and 3rd on successive days. In the month of October, he ran four times in 28 days and won twice and was second once.

However, the two races that stand out that year were ones that he didn't win. In early December, at Warwick, he was three lengths third, getting 8lbs, to ESB, winner of a famous Grand National the following year.

Later that month, just after Christmas, I saw Dad ride Polonius in at Cheltenham, my first visit there. I well understood it to be much more important than our local East Midlands courses. I thought my father looked truly splendid in his royal blue and white colours, a jersey not a silk jacket. His royal blue silk cap was worn over a skullcap that was made of a thin layer of resin cork that provided little protection compared to modern helmets and didn't even have a chin strap.

Dad and Polonius finished a decent third in a four-mile Fred Withington Chase. Much Obliged, winner of the inaugural Whitbread Gold Cup two years later was 15 lengths behind him in sixth place. Several of the runners featured in the following year's Grand National. The winner, Must, was favourite for the National, but fell at the first. Armorial III, who was second at Cheltenham, led at Aintree until he

My father, Colin Hailstone, on Polonius – racecourse not known

fell at the 26th fence. M'As-Tu Vu, the Queen Mother's horse, finished just behind Polonius at Cheltenham but fell at the 19th in the National.

It is hard to believe when I am at Cheltenham nowadays, that my first visit to the home of National Hunt racing was two-thirds of a century ago.

Along with those successes in 1955 there were two races, at Buckfastleigh and at Huntingdon, in which Polonius's race ended with him running out. Running out was to be as common a feature of his racecourse visits as winning. In the years from 1955 to 1958, he ran out on no fewer than ten occasions (almost 15% of his races). My father always said that he was a tricky horse to ride. He raced well off the pace and took quite a bit of getting going. He also tended to down tools when he got to the head of affairs. It is notable that he was second exactly the same number of times that he won. He was always running on strongly in the closing stages and I suppose that sometimes he got there a bit too soon and, on other occasions, not quite early enough. A further sign that he was not always focused on the job in hand is that he was always fitted with blinkers.

1956 – Aintree

The 1956 Grand National is almost universally known as Devon Loch's, with a few remembering is as ESB's race but, for me, it will always be Polonius's National.

Following Polonius's good showing at Cheltenham over a marathon distance against serious National horses, Dad set his sights on Aintree. 1956 began with an indifferent run at Leicester, close second to the odds-on favourite at Market Rasen and another run-out at Newbury. He may have run out early in the race because he raced again the following day, at Worcester, this time with Tim Brookshaw as his jockey, again not making the frame. The Worcester race was exactly three weeks before the National.

About ten days after the Worcester outing, with Aintree less than a fortnight off, disaster struck. Dad and I were at home on a Saturday afternoon. My mother and sister had gone shopping in Market Harborough. A piteous noise penetrated the house from across the lane. When we went out to investigate, we found that a calf had walked into the pond and got herself stuck in the mud. She was in a panic with her head not far above the water. Dad waded in to pull her out, only to discover that she was too deep into the mud. Even with a rope and head collar, we couldn't extricate her. My father was able to prevent her from drowning only by standing in the freezing water for about an hour until my mother returned. With a tractor and rope we freed her but my father ended up with severe pneumonia. It probably didn't help that he had been wasting for several weeks to get down to the 10lb 3oz that Polonius was to carry at Aintree.

In the event, Dad was too ill even to go to Aintree to watch the race. He was quite crushed with disappointment, which, if only I had been twelve instead of nine, could have been avoided, as I would have been able to bring the tractor round to save the calf.

It is disappointing that, having been witness to one of the best-known

National Hunt races of the last century, my memories of it are hazy - compared, for example, with my visit to Sandown Park the following year. This may be because I sensed my mother's great anxiety about Dad's medical condition. In later years she told me that his fever was very bad and that Dr Pickering had arranged to admit him to hospital, only for my father to decline to take his advice.

In the event, we left him in the care of my very capable Aunt Nellie, the wife of Dad's younger brother, Ant, who was working on our farm at that time. Ant and Nellie lived in the cottage next door to our house.

We travelled to Aintree with George Burnham in his large Austin 16. Burnham's style of driving owed something to Mr Toad, and he was the sort of man who may well have worn special driving garments. Mum had passed her driving test only a few months earlier. She was a very nervous driver and, with Burnham at the wheel, probably a nervous passenger too. From the back seat I heard her urging him to slow down quite a few times.

George Burnham possessed a slightly ramshackle but serviceable horse box in which Polonius habitually went racing but, on this occasion, I think he was driven by Mr Simkins, the garagiste of Hallaton who transported horses as a side line. He also possessed an ancient Rolls Royce, which, although principally for weddings, also served as a rather glamorous taxi, when carless people in those parts needed to go to Harborough railway station. I think that Polonius was accompanied on his journey north by Joyce Noble and her sister's fiancé, Jack Mason. They were certainly there, when we arrived at Aintree on the morning of the great race.

We spent the night in an hotel somewhere north of Stoke. This would have been my first experience of such an establishment, except for summer holidays in Sheringham in Norfolk and the Sunnylands there was more boarding house than hotel. I remember being given supper in Mum's and my room while she and Burnham ate in the hotel's dining room. We made the return trip without an overnight stop arriving home very late. Polonius did not reach Belcher's Lodge until Sunday.

My strongest memory of Aintree is of the huge mass of humanity gathered there and the deafening noise in the closing stages of the races. I had never seen a crowd nearly so large. Viewing for owners and trainers was on the roof of the County Stand and I well remember cheering Polonius as he jumped the Chair at the end of the first circuit, still going but well back in the field.

I have often been asked whether I remember seeing Devon Loch's belly flop. The honest answer is that I don't know. One has seen the film so many times over the last sixty years. I do remember the huge sense of shock, horror and confusion, although, we were mainly concerned to get down to ground level and make sure that Polonius was Okay.

It is impossible to say how much difference, if any, it would have made had Dad been able to ride Polonius in the National. My father certainly had developed an understanding of and sympathy for this not very straightforward horse. No other rider ever won a National Hunt race on him. The first and only time Gene Kelly sat on Polonius was in the paddock at Aintree and he had never ridden a horse over the National fences, and of course these were the old Aintree obstacles, very solid, very upright and very uncompromising. It seems that, very late in the day, Dad was still hoping, probably unrealistically, to be well enough to ride him. Gene told me that he was only given the ride the day before the race. My father was in the race card as Polonius's jockey.

Gene Kelly grew up, not in the emerald isle but in the West Midlands and neither was he a dancer. He served his apprenticeship with Joe Lawson, Polonius's erstwhile trainer, towards the end of the War at the famous Manton stables in Wiltshire but, after National Service (where he was United Services flyweight and bantamweight boxing champion), he gravitated towards the National Hunt code. He had his first winner less than two years before the 1956 National, so Polonius was not in the hands of a seasoned campaigner.

Gene Kelly riding Queen Elizabeth the Queen Mother's Gay Record

THIRD RACE   About four miles   **BLUE BADGE**
and 856 yards

3-15 The GRAND NATIONAL STEEPLE CHASE

(Handicap) of 10 sov. each, 50 sov. extra if left in after Tuesday, January 31st, with an additional **40** sov. if left in after Tuesday, March 6th, with **6000** sov. (including a trophy value **500 sov.**) added; second to receive 10%, third 5%, and fourth 2½% of the whole stakes ; **for six yrs old and upwards** *which, up to or on the day of closing, have been placed first, second, or third by the Judge in a steeple chase of any distance at Aintree, Liverpool (this does not include such steeple chases run at the December Meeting on the Mildmay Course), or which have won a steeple chase of three miles or upwards of the advertised value of 300 sov., or with at least 250 sov. added to a sweepstakes (or the equivalent in foreign distances and money), or which have won any steeplechase value 400 sov. to the winner (or the equivalent in foreign money), selling races in every case excepted ;* weights published January 26th at noon : the highest weight to be not more than 12st. 7lb, and the lowest weight not less than 10st ; the **GRAND NATIONAL COURSE, about four miles and 856 yards.**

Declaration of forfeit to Messrs. Weatherby and Sons only. 61 entries, 60 sov. forfeit declared for 9 and 10 sov. forfeit declared for 13. Closed January 3rd, 1956.

.*. The trainer of the winner will receive a Cup value **50 sov.** and the rider of the winner a Cup value **25 sov.**

There will be a Parade for this race.

VALUE TO WINNER £8,695 5s. 0d.

Jockey		Age	st.	lb.	Colours	Trainer
B. Marshall	1 **EARLY MIST** Mr. John Dunlop ch g Brumeux—Sudden Dawn	11	12	2	Green and yellow (hlvd), slvs reversed, green cap	B. Marshall
T. Taaffe	2 **ROYAL TAN** Prince Aly Khan ch g Tartan—Princess of Birds	12	12	1	Green, red sash, green cap	M. V. O'Brien (In Ireland)
P. Taaffe	3 **QUARE TIMES** Mrs. W. H. E. Welman b g Artist's Son—Lavenco	10	11	12	Red, white and blue hps, blue slvs, red cap	M. V. O'Brien (In Ireland)
R. Emery	4 **MARINER'S LOG** The Late Ld. Bicester ch g Archive—She Gone	9	11	11	Black, gold slvs, red cap	G. Beeby
R. Francis	5 **DEVON LOCH** Queen Elizabeth b or br g Devonian—Coolaleen	10	11	4	Blue, buff stripes, blue slvs, black cap, gold tassel	P. Cazalet
F. Winter	6 **SUNDEW** Mrs. Geoffrey Kohn ch g Sun King—Parsonstown	10	11	4	Flame, emerald green sleeves, flame cuffs	F. Hudson
D. V. Dick	7 **E.S.B.** Mrs. Leonard Carver b or br g Bidar—English Summer	10	11	3	Green, white hoop and armlets	T. F. Rimell
A. P. Thompson	8 **HIGH GUARD** Mr. J. A. Keith gr g Fishguard—High Places	9	11	1	Brown, light blue slvs and cap	N. Crump
H. J. East	9 **MUCH OBLIGED** Mr. H. Draper bl or br g Cameron—May Sen	8	11	0	Red and white (halved), slvs reversed, check cap	N. Crump
Mr. R. Brewis	10 **DUNBOY II** Mrs. M. Bruce ch g Piuxit—Gaiety	12	11	0	Saxe blue and white (halved), blue collar and sleeves, quartered cap	J. S. Wight
R. Turnell	11 **CAREY'S COTTAGE** Col. W. H. Whitbread b g Uncle Willie—Halo	9	10	13	Chocolate, yellow collar, cuffs and cap	G. Balding

Continued on next page.

Jockey			Age	st.	lb.	Colours	Trainer
J. Dowdeswell	12	**ARMORIAL III** Mme. K. Hennessy b g Souverain—Skiperai	7	10	10	Straw, chocolate hoop	F. Walwyn
L. McMorrow	13	**MERRY WINDSOR** Mr. I. Holliday b g Foxlight—Courcelle	8	10	10	Yellow, red and green quartered cap	D. Doyle
R. Morrow	14	**MUST** Mrs. W. L. Pilkington b g Umidkhan—Cadamstown Lass	8	10	10	Dark blue, light blue hoop and slvs, white cap	A. S. Kilpatrick
T. Molony	15	**KEY ROYAL** Mr. A. H. Birtwistle b g Royal Charger—Keyboard	8	10	8	Maroon, yellow hpd slvs, check cap	W. Stephenson
A. Freeman	16	**M'AS-TU-VU** Queen Elizabeth br g Pampeiro—Malle Post	10	10	6	Blue, buff stripes, blue slvs, white cap	P. Cazalet
Mr. C. Pocock	17	**REVEREND PRINCE** Mr. P. Dufosee b g His Reverence—Princess Pat	10	10	5	Khaki, dark green cross belts, black cap	P. Dufosee
P. A. Farrell	18	**WITTY** Mr. Clifford Nicholson br g Foroughi—Brown Wings	11	10	4	Grey, scarlet slvs, collar, braid and cap	W. Hall
D. Ancil	19	**DOMATA** Mr. E. Stanning b g Domaha—Sunita	10	10	4	Canary, light blue slvs, check cap	F. Cundell
Mr. C. Hailstone	20	**POLONIUS** Mrs. D. Hailstone ch g Epigram—Charmain	10	10	3	Blue, white hoop, blue sleeves and cap	G. Burnham
R. J. Hamey	21	**ATHENIAN** Col. W. H. Whitbread br g The Phoenix—Felorbia	7	10	3	Chocolate, yellow collar, cuffs and cap	G. Balding
Mr. J. Straker	22	**GENTLE MOYA** Mr. J. J. Straker b m Steel-point—Laura Gay	10	10	2	Scarlet, green hoop, white cap	C. Bewicke
C. Finnegan	23	**NO RESPONSE** Sir Thomas Ainsworth br m Iceberg II—Water Gypsy	10	10	1	Blue, red hoop	J. Osborne (In Ireland)
J. A. Bullock	24	**CLEARING** Mr. M. Kingsley b g Labrador—Celimene VI	9	10	1	Black and pink (qtd), pink cap	W. Stephenson
A. Oughton	25	**EAGLE LODGE** Mr. N. A. Mardon b g Jamaica Inn—Mountain Side	7	10	0	Dark blue, two pale green diagonal stripes, and hoop on cap	M. Feakes
N. Wilkinson	26	**ONTRAY** Capt. Scott Briggs br g Legend of France—Guinea Fowl	8	10	0	Primrose	L. S. Briggs
J. Cuddihy	27	**VICTORY MORN** Mr. John Dixon br g Pane Beg—Market Bar	12	10	0	Yellow, brown and yellow qtd cap	J. Dixon
A. Grantham	28	**WILD WISDOM** Mr. E. Foster br g Perion—Miss Fix-It	11	10	0	Grey, Royal blue hoop on body	J. Ford
P. Major	29	**BORDER LUCK** Mr. J. R. Bower bl g Squadron Castle or Port of Call— Luck	11	10	0	Gold and green (halved), nigger brown cap	J. R. Bower
J. Power	30	**PIPPYKIN** Mr. R. D. Darragh ch g Escamillo—Relizane	8	10	0	Black, scarlet slvs and sash, qtd cap	S. Parker
S. Mellor	31	**MARTINIQUE** Mr. A. Greenberg b g Mieuxce—Carruse	10	10	0	White, green sleeves and sash, qtd cap	G. R. Owen
	32	**VENETIAN LAW** Mr. M. L. Marsh b m Within-the-Law—Lady Wick	9	10	0	Violet and white check, white cap	M. L. Marsh
K. Maudsley	33	**SUN CLASP** Mr. E. O. Boardman b g Sol Oriens—Buckle	8	10	0	White, dark green slvs, hooped cap	K. Maudsley

Polonius was not a quick horse and won his races by staying on strongly, usually from way off the pace. Gene says that they just went too fast for him in the early stages and that he was never in a position to get involved on the second circuit. The going was on the quick side of good and the time of the race, at a shade over 9 minutes 21 seconds was very fast for that era. In fact, the race had only been completed in a faster time on three occasions since 1900 and two of those were Golden Miller and Reynoldstown. It would be another 17 years until Red Rum ran the race faster than ESB had.

Nevertheless, for a 66/1 bar shot, Polonius acquitted himself reasonably well. When, very tired, he refused at the 26th (the fence after Valentine's) only 12 of the 29 runners were still in the race.

More than forty years later, I found myself at a pre-National meeting of Chris Pitt's West Midland's Racing Club. A dapper man, appearing to be in his seventies, with twinkling eyes, short of stature even measured against others who rode racehorses for a living, stood before me as I returned from the bar and asked me whether I was 'Colin's boy'. Following that initial encounter, I developed a most enjoyable friendship with Gene and his charming and funny wife, Diana. I visited them often at their house near Broadway and they came to our box at Cheltenham at least once most seasons. On the morning of the 2015 Grand National I phoned Gene to tell him that we had a horse in the race that day. He wanted to know why a Hailstone runner in that great race had been offered to another jockey. He may even have done better than James Best, who came off Gas Line Boy at the first.

Gene suffered a bad stroke in 2017 and was pretty much housebound but he watched racing every day on TV and loved to reminisce about his days in the saddle, especially the races he won on the Queen Mother's Gay Record and the evening he danced with her at her party at the Savoy, held to celebrate her 100th winner. He died in January 2020, aged 91.

Following the Grand National my father rode Polonius four times at Midlands courses, with indifferent results. But my mother always said that he started working and riding again too soon after his illness. During the summer he had a serious relapse and was in bed for many weeks. He didn't ride in a race again for close to a year.

Neither was he capable of training Polonius, who spent the 1956/57 winter in the yard of George Vergette in Market Deeping, Lincolnshire, where he was ridden by stable jockey Geoff Mann and by Tommy Shone. Polonius carried neither of them to victory but over a couple of months from December to February, Shone was second twice and third twice on him. One of the second placed finishes was the four mile Fred Withington Chase at Cheltenham, in which he had finished third the previous winter. The record shows that, typically, he came strongly off the pace to take the lead going over the last but was headed on the run in.

1957 – the first Whitbread

Dad rode Polonius again towards the end of March and, in April, he came back to Belcher's Lodge. At the end of that month he ran in the first Whitbread Gold Cup at Sandown Park.

With the exception of summer forays to Devon, Polonius raced mainly in the Midlands and North. Sandown had considerably more prestige than most of the courses at which he had competed. Opened in 1875, it was the first racecourse to be designed as a leisure destination. Trains from central London were fast and frequent, and the course had been laid out in a natural amphitheatre, making for excellent viewing from the enclosures. In fact, unlike other courses at that time, the only practical way to watch the racing was to pay an entry fee.

From its earliest days, Sandown hosted both flat and National Hunt racing. The Eclipse Stakes, still its most prestigious flat race, started in 1886, but the peripatetic four mile National Hunt Chase, now part of the Cheltenham Festival, was run at the new Esher course in its opening year. There are now five Grade 1 National Hunt races in Sandown's calendar. It is a superb test for steeplechasers, requiring not only great stamina to meet the demands of the sharp uphill finish and 220 yard run from the last, but also the athletic ability to jump eleven fences per circuit, including the three railway fences in the back straight that require an extraordinarily good and accurate jumping rhythm.

The Whitbread was an early example of commercial sponsorship in British sport. Indeed, it may have been the first National Hunt race to be sponsored. The Chairman of Whitbread at that time, Colonel Bill Whitbread, was a keen amateur jockey and had ridden twice in the Grand National. His company continued to sponsor the race for 44 years, until 2001. Over those years it was won by some famous names including Pas Seul, Arkle, Mill House, and Desert Orchid.

The considerable prize offered by the Whitbread brewery (more valuable than the Cheltenham Gold Cup that year) attracted a first-class field that included a Grand National winner, Sundew and no less than three past and future Cheltenham Gold Cup winners in Mandarin, Linwell and Gay Donald. In the contest too was Lucky Dome, who, a few years earlier had been one of the horses whose 'inconsistent running' had given allegedly jealous and resentful Irish Turf Club stewards a reason to withdraw Vincent O'Brien's training licence for three months.

In that first running, on firm ground, Much Obliged prevailed in a very close finish over Mandarin with the rest of the field well behind. There were 24 runners, of which Polonius was 12th of 17 finishers.

Before the 2017 race, I was standing looking up at the board, just beyond the weighing room, that bears the names of all the Whitbread winners, when a young racing journalist acquaintance asked me why I was looking so pensive. He was almost disbelieving when I told him that I was thinking about having been there sixty years previously to watch my father ride in the first Whitbread.

My memories of that day are quite strong, considering that I was only ten. Nowadays the drive from Horninghold to Esher would take well under three hours but on 1957 roads in a lorry, it could easily have been double that. My father had found that Polonius performed better when he had done a little gentle work in the morning of race days. He was also a somewhat fretful traveller. So, after his morning work on the day before the race, he was loaded Into George Burnham's lorry in which he and my father took him down to spend the night in the Sandown stables. Burnham had a keen interest in Polonius's career and, to be fair to him, never showed the least resentment that Dad had got such good value for his £25 and the hay. More often than not, Polonius travelled in his vehicle.

My mother's confidence was certainly not strong enough to permit her to drive to London, so, early on Saturday morning, we drove to Market Harborough to get the train to St Pancras, followed by another train from Waterloo to Esher, where we walked across the course to meet Dad and Burnham. This was the first time that I had ever been to London and I think that was more exciting than watching Polonius race at Sandown. After all, I had seen him in a fair few races by that time.

I was particularly fascinated by the Tube and rather apprehensive about the escalators. Some years earlier I had been given a book entitled *The Thinsies.* It was about what happens to people who fail to step off the escalator. They get sucked down and flattened in the process and live in the land of the Thinsies beneath the escalators.

My recollection is that none of us expected Polonius to win and that Dad was pleased that he completed. He was only getting a pound from Mandarin!

In the 1950s race meetings that had flat and National Hunt Races on the same card were quite common, although now Swinton Hurdle at Haydock is the only one that survives. Whitbread day was one, as was the Grand National card. One of the highlights of that day at Sandown was watching Lester Piggott ride two winners.

Other memories of that day are that the race was televised (Polonius's only TV race) and, most excitingly of all, that I was allowed to travel home in the lorry. I well remember stopping towards dusk at a pub somewhere on the Great North Road that had a paddock. I held the leading rein while Polonius grazed and Dad and Burnham took refreshment inside for what seemed like a very long time.

Another purple patch

Two weeks after Sandown, Polonius was back at Towcester, in less exalted company, at the beginning of another purple patch. Over the next five months, from twelve starts, he clocked up four wins, two seconds, three thirds and a fourth. He pulled up and ran out in the other two. Over seven days in south Devon in August, he was first and second at Newton Abbot and ran out at Buckfastleigh.

By this time Dad was riding as a professional. In those days the Jockey Club was anxious that 'gentlemen riders' should not be seen to be taking the bread out of the mouths of those who earned livings as jockeys, and, as by the end of the 1956/57 season my father had ridden seven winners, he was asked to apply for a professional licence.

In November that year, Polonius ran in the valuable three-mile Cowley Novices' Hurdle at Cheltenham with George Vergette on his back. This is the only hurdle race he ran under our ownership and the only time George Vergette rode him. In a huge field, he finished 17th of the 35 runners.

Polonius with Dad – racecourse unknown

December was not a very successful end of the year for Polonius. The record of his last three races shows that he ran out, fell and was pulled up. The fall, at Southwell, was one of only three such mishaps in his National Hunt career. He had previously fallen at Nottingham under Geoff Mann and was to do so again at Southwell in 1958.

However, in his first race in December 1957, at Leicester, he was a close second to a horse named Captain Courage. Polonius finished very strongly in a five-runner race, just failing by a neck to get up

Frank Gilman, East Midlands farmer, owner/trainer of Grittar and Chairman of the Old Stamfordians

to win. The odds on favourite was Tiberetta, a wonderful mare bred and trained by Edward Courage. She won the Becher Chase and the Grand Sefton at Aintree and was third, second and fourth in consecutive Nationals in the late Fifties. After her racing career, she gave birth to the great Spanish Steps.

That Leicester race sticks in my memory because the winner was owned by Frank Gilman. My father got on fairly well with Frank and his brothers, all East Midlands farmers, but my mother did not care for Frank at all. Even at the tender age of ten, I could see that congratulating Frank, as the horses came back, was something of a struggle for Mum.

In later years, after we had moved back to Carberry Farm, my grandfather's place in Northamptonshire, Frank Gilman purchased Belcher's Lodge from the Brudenell family. His horses were often at grass there, including Grittar, with whom he won the 1982 Grand National.

Frank Gilman and I went to the same school albeit several decades apart. When I was chairman of the old boys' club, about fifteen years ago, I was asked to give a talk to some of the Upper VIth boys. They asked me some questions, one of which was whether I had any unfulfilled ambitions. My answer, without hesitation, was that I still hoped to be the second Chairman of the Old Stamfordians to own a Grand National winner. I have not given up hope.

The legacy of Polonius

1958 was the last year of Polonius's racing career and of his life. Maybe he was feeling his age, as it was not his best. He completed only four of his twelve starts although, in those, he recorded a win, a second and a fourth. When he won, at Towcester in May, he beat Captain Courage, who was 19lbs worse off this time, and also Four Ten, from whom he was getting almost two stone.

Four Ten was another horse with an unusual career. He was a hunter, also trained by his farmer owner, who did well in a few point-to-points and a hunter chase and then, as a seven-year-old, was sent to be trained professionally for National Hunt races. He won the National Hunt Chase in 1953 at Cheltenham and the Gold Cup the following year on very heavy ground, and many other good chases.

In Polonius's last race at Leicester in early December, he finished second with Captain Courage behind him again. Three weeks later he died. He had probably burst his pulmonary artery. His body was collected by the Woodland Pytchley kennels.

Dad first rode Polonius in a race in June 1955 and in 49 more over the next three and a half years. Six other jockeys rode him in 17 races. From his total of 67 races in those years, the record shows that Polonius won 10 races, was second ten times, third eight times, fourth four times – and he ran out 10 times! My father was the only rider to win on him.

Dad survived Polonius by just short of twenty years, succumbing to lung cancer at only 59. So many of our conversations were about horses and racing. The night before he died in July 1977 he said that he thought The Minstrel would win the following Saturday's King George and Queen Elizabeth Stakes. I went to Ascot of course and my sadness was very slightly relieved, to see Dad's prediction prevail when Lester Piggott got the chesnut son of Northern Dancer with his four flashy white stockings up to win in the dying strides of the race.

Dad always said that the Polonius years were the best of his life and, indeed, they were hugely exciting for the whole family. There were always ponies and horses around from the earliest times I can remember and racing was part of everyday life and conversation, so I was destined to have a strong interest in horses. However, I think that, more than anything, I owe my lifelong passion for horse racing to my involvement with Polonius during those impressionable years from six to eleven years old.

I am grateful to have known him.